★ IT'S MY STATE! ★

IOWA

David C. King

Cavendish
Square

New York

Published in 2014 by Cavendish Square Publishing, LLC
303 Park Avenue South, Suite 1247, New York, NY 10010

Library of Congress Cataloging-in-Publication Data

King, David C.
Iowa / David C. King.
    pages cm. — (It's my state)
Includes index.
ISBN 978-1-62712-222-1 (hardcover) ISBN 978-1-62712-480-5 (paperback) ISBN 978-1-62712-233-7 (ebook)
1. Iowa—Juvenile literature. I. Title.

F621.3.K563 2014
977.7—dc23

2013030181

This edition developed for Cavendish Square Publishing by RJF Publishing LLC (www.RJFpublishing.com)
Series Designer, Second Edition: Tammy West/Westgraphix LLC
Editorial Director: Dean Miller
Editor: Sara Howell
Copy Editor: Cynthia Roby
Art Director: Jeffrey Talbot
Layout Design: Erica Clendening
Production Manager: Jennifer Ryder-Talbot

Maps, illustrations, and graphics © Cavendish Square Publishing, LLC.
Illustrations and map on page 6 by Christopher Santoro
Map on page 76 by Ian Worpole

The photographs in this book are used by permission and through the courtesy of: Cover (main) JenniferPhotographyImaging/Getty Images; cover (inset) Katrina Wittkamp/Getty Images; p. 4 (top) Photo Researchers, Inc.: Kenneth M. Highfill; p. 4 (bottom) Steve Maslowski; p. 5 (top) Joseph SohmVisions of America/Photodisc/Getty Images; p. 5 (bottom) Mark A. Schneider; p. 8 Alex Maclean/Getty Images; p. 9 Julie Habel; pp. 10, 31 Joseph Sohm/ChromoSohm Inc.; p. 11, 13, 74 Tom Bean; p. 14 The Image Works: Andre Jenny; p. 16 Michael Leach/Getty Images; p. 17 Gregory K. Scott; pp. 19, 26, 56 Ty Smedes Nature; p. 20 Photography Michael P. Gadomski; p. 21 (top) Rod Planck; p. 21 (bottom) Art Wolfe/Getty Images; pp. 22, 73 (top) Corbis; pp. 25, 27, 30 Northwind Pictures; pp. 26, 32, 33, 35, 38, 52, 53, 58, 70 Getty Images; p. 29 Tim Thompson; pp. 39, 50 (top), 52 (bottom) Bettmann; p. 40 Lake County Museum; p. 42 The Washington Post/Getty Images; p. 44 Craig Aurness; p. 46 Lindsay Hebberd; p. 47 Hulton-Deutsch Collection; pp. 49, 65 age footstock; p. 50 (bottom) Chris Polk; p. 51 (top) AFP/Getty Images; pp. 54, 67 Walter Bibikow; p. 57 MCT via Getty Images; p. 62 Annie Griffiths Belt; p. 66 Envision: Mark Ferri; p. 68 Steven Rubin; p. 69 Envision: Mark Ferri; p. 72 Richard Cummins; p. 73 (bottom) Scott Camazine.

Every effort has been made to locate the copyright holders of the images used in this book.

Printed in the United States of America.

CONTENTS

State Flower: Wild Rose

The wild rose was selected as the state flower in 1897, though no specific type of wild rose was singled out. However, many Iowans think of the wild prairie rose as the state flower. These prairie roses are found throughout the state. They bloom from June to late summer in different shades of pink. In the past, pioneers heading west in late spring often decorated their wagons with the colorful blossoms.

State Bird: Eastern Goldfinch

The Eastern goldfinch is sometimes called the American goldfinch. These birds make their homes throughout the state. A male Eastern goldfinch has bright yellow feathers on most of its body and black feathers on its head and wings. Female goldfinches are usually yellow and brown. The Eastern goldfinch was made the state bird in 1933.

State Tree: Oak

The Iowa state legislature chose the oak as the state tree in 1961. Different types of oak trees thrive throughout the state. Many wild animals make their homes in the trees. Oaks also provide food for a variety of Iowa's animals. Residents have long used oak to make products such as furniture.

Capital City: Des Moines

Des Moines was founded in 1843. It covers an area just over 80 square miles (207 sq km) and has a population of 206,559 people. Des Moines became the capital of Iowa in 1857. Des Moines is a center of culture in Iowa, with history and art museums, a botanical garden and zoo, a symphony, and many performing arts groups.

Highest Point: Hawkeye Point

Iowa's highest point lies just 3.5 miles (5.6 km) from the state's northern border with Minnesota. Hawkeye Point reaches 1,670 feet (510 m). Hawkeye Point features an information kiosk, granite markers, and signs pointing to the highest points in the other 49 states.

State Rock: Geode

Geodes are hard-shelled rocks with mineral crystals inside. Many of these rocks are found in limestone formations throughout Iowa. The crystals inside the geodes were formed over thousands of years as water dripped on the limestone.

IOWA

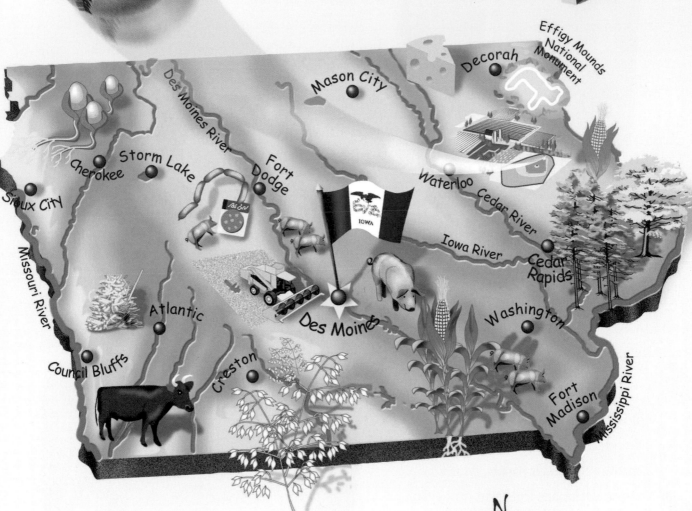

Effigy Mounds National Monument

Decorah

Mason City

Des Moines River

Storm Lake

Cherokee

Sioux City

Fort Dodge

Waterloo

Cedar River

Iowa River

Cedar Rapids

Missouri River

Atlantic

Des Moines

IOWA

Washington

Council Bluffs

Creston

Fort Madison

Mississippi River

N

W   E

S

The Hawkeye State

People often think of Iowa as a flatland covered with many farms devoted to raising corn, cattle, and hogs. That is an accurate description, but it is not complete. While it is true that 90 percent of the state's land is farmland, Iowa also has areas of rolling hills, towering bluffs, valleys, forests, rivers, and lakes. The landscape is also dotted with cities, towns, and villages.

In a number of ways, Iowa is a state that is in the middle. In geographic terms, for example, the state is in the middle of the United States. The Mississippi River, which forms Iowa's eastern border, divides the nation into east and west.

Iowa is also in a middle position in terms of size and population. The state covers a land area of 55,857 square miles (144,669 sq km), making it twenty-third in size when it is compared to all the other states. In population, Iowa has more than three million people. This means that on average, there are 54.5 people for every 1 square mile (2.6 sq km) in the state. This is called the population density. Thirty-four states have a higher population density than Iowa, and 15 have lower population densities.

Quick Facts

Iowa's Borders

North	Minnesota
South	Missouri
East	Mississippi River
	Wisconsin
	Illinois
West	Missouri River
	Nebraska

Iowa has many wide, open spaces that are perfect for farming.

The Land

Tens of thousands of years ago, the land that now includes Iowa was shaped by an Ice Age, or a period when glaciers, or great sheets of ice, slowly moved down over much of the continent. The moving glaciers created lakes, leveled hills, and pushed around massive amounts of soil and rock. These giant glaciers are the reason why Iowa can be divided into three geographic regions.

The northeastern region of what is now Iowa was covered by only one glacier, so it was not affected by the force of the ice as much as the rest of the state was. The central region, which covers more than half of the state's area, is the most level region. There, the melting glacier left behind deep, rich soil. The third region, which makes up the western and southern fringes of present-day Iowa, has soil that was blown so hard and for so long by the winds that it was turned into hills and ridges.

An unpaved road cuts through a forest in northeastern Iowa.

Northeastern Iowa

Visitors who enter Iowa through the northeastern corner might be surprised to see a landscape that has more hills and forests than flat cornfields and hog farms. Bordered by the majestic span of the Mississippi River, this northeastern land also has river valleys and wooded hills of oak, maple, elm, and other trees. In the fall, these wooded areas sport reds, oranges, and yellows as the leaves change colors.

This part of Iowa also has sections of rugged hills and bluffs that rise 300 to 400 feet (91–122 m) above the Mississippi. Wildlife and fish refuges dot the river area. The river valley is also part of the Mississippi Flyway—the great migration route for birds moving north in summer and south in winter. Enormous flocks of Canada geese, snow geese, sandhill cranes, and other birds flap to noisy landings in Iowa's protected areas along the river.

Long, winding rivers, which rise in the prairie lands of central Iowa, flow in a southeasterly direction into the Mississippi River. Several of these rivers carve deep gorges as they near the Mississippi.

Throughout Iowa's history, many communities, such as Bellevue, were established along the Mississippi River.

Des Moines has the largest population among all of Iowa's towns and cities. This capital city is home to the state government and to many thriving businesses.

North-Central Iowa

The glaciers that moved south into the north-central area of Iowa produced a flat landscape that creates the picture of Iowa as a land of endless cornfields. The deep soil deposited by the retreating ice sheet is said to be among the most fertile soil in the world. This makes it perfect for growing crops.

This landscape is part of the Great Plains region of North America. These plains extend from western Iowa to the Rocky Mountains a couple of states away. Until the late 1800s, great herds of bison roamed this prairie land, moving north from Mexico to Canada. As pioneer settlers from the East and from Europe moved to the prairie, the wild grassland was replaced with wheat and corn crops. Wild bison herds disappeared due to hunting and loss of natural grazing land. The Great Plains eventually became the place where the world's largest supply of grain was produced.

A ridge that runs across this region of Iowa—from northwest to southeast—is called the Missouri-Mississippi Divide. Rivers on the west of the divide flow west into the Missouri River. Rivers on the east flow southeast into the Mississippi River. The longest of Iowa's rivers, the Des Moines River, flows 485 miles (781 km) through the center of the state. The state capital, Des Moines, which is also Iowa's largest city, is located on both banks of the Des Moines River.

Western and Southern Iowa

Wrapped around the north-central region of Iowa to the west is the third region, which geologists call the Dissected Till Plains. The first of the four great ice sheets that once covered Iowa left behind huge quantities of till, or layers of soil and rocks. Over thousands of years, after the ice sheet had disappeared, streams cut through, or dissected, the plains. Glacial movement over time also created bodies of water.

The wind also helped to shape this region. Wind pushed soil up against the Missouri River, forming bluffs that rise 100 to 300 feet (30–91 m) above the river. The soil here is deeper than anywhere else in the world, except for a river valley in China. These types of land formations are called loess hills. Because of years of wind and water moving around the soil and land, Iowa's loess hills are rough, jagged, and strangely shaped in some places. There are stair-like landforms and even some that look like parts of an animal's body.

The northwestern parts of the state are also home to a number of small lakes. Larger lakes, such as Storm Lake, are popular spots for fishing, boating, and other water sports. Major cities in western Iowa include Council Bluffs and Sioux City.

Climate

Iowa has a continental climate, which is a climate that is found in the interior of Earth's different continents. More simply, a continental climate has cold winters and warm, humid summers. However, there are variations in climate within the state.

Loess is often pronounced like "less" or "luss."

In May 2013, a snowstorm swept across the north-central United States. The storm, called Winter Storm Achilles, caused 11 inches (28 cm) of snow to fall in parts of Iowa, breaking the record for the most snowfall in May. Just a couple of weeks later, temperatures reached over 100°F (37.7°C) in some parts of the state!

For instance, the northwest has cold January winters, with an average temperature of 14°F (-10°C). In the southeast, though, the average January temperature is 22°F (-5.5°C).

Throughout the state, warm July days have an average temperature of 74°F (23°C). The state also gets a good deal of rainfall in the summer. Precipitation, which takes the form of rain when it is warm and snow, sleet, or freezing rain when it is cold, is usually four times greater in June than in the

Iowans enjoy sunny summer days on the state's lakes.

winter months. Rain also varies according to different regions. Each year, the northwest gets about 28 inches (71 cm) compared to the southeast's 35 inches (89 cm). Snowfall shows a similar difference, with an average of 50 inches (127 cm) of snow per year in the north compared to 22 inches (56 cm) a year in southern Iowa.

Weather changes can occur rapidly, and even Iowans are sometimes surprised by sudden changes. Sometimes the temperature can rise or fall many degrees in a day. A burst of cold air from the northwest can cause a sudden drop in temperature, while warm air can bring a sudden blast of hot air along with heavy thunderstorms.

Wildlife

In the early years of settlement by pioneers from the East and from Europe, the newcomers stayed in the eastern region of the state. There, the forests provided lumber for homes, while the rivers were used for water and transportation. During this time, the settlers and their descendants leveled many of the forests by cutting down most of the trees.

In spite of so much woodland being destroyed, Iowa still has about 1,500,000 acres (607,028 ha) of forest. Hardwood trees, such as maple, oak, hickory, and walnut, grow in the river valleys. The hardwoods not only produce the spectacular colors of autumn, but also provide homes and food for Iowa wildlife. They are also used for fine furniture. Evergreens, such as white fir, white and Norway spruce, and red and jack pines, are common in the state. Red cedar, one of the only evergreens native to Iowa, is found along the Cedar River. Farther west, cottonwoods and willows are fairly common along the rivers.

An attractive sight in the spring is the burst of wildflowers that blanket Iowa's prairie grasslands. From March to October, Iowa's roadsides also have colorful blossoms. The blooming display begins with violets, marsh marigolds, and bloodroots. Summer flowers include prairie lilies, purple phlox, and wild roses. Autumn is the time for prairie aster, goldenrod, sunflowers, and gentians.

Grey partridges feed in soybean fields during the summer, then move to cornfields in the fall.

Many migrating birds like to build their nests in fields, rather than in trees. The open farmlands of Iowa provide excellent nesting grounds. Quail, partridge, and pheasant have plenty of grain to feed on as they nest among the corn, hay, or oats. An Iowa state hatchery in Boone County raises these species to be released into the wild as game birds, which are birds designated to be hunted. Enormous flocks of winter fowl—ducks and geese—cross Iowa by either the Missouri River or the Mississippi flyway.

White-tailed deer are still plentiful in the state, as are coyotes, foxes, and opossums. Smaller animals, like rabbits, squirrels, and chipmunks are common in wooded areas. Fast-moving streams are well stocked with bass and trout. Lakes and slower streams contain fish such as largemouth bass, bluegills, crappies, northern pike, and walleyes.

Restoring the Environment

Many Iowans have long been concerned about the state's land, water, and wildlife. In the mid-twentieth century, a large number of Iowans decided that they were not pleased with what was happening to the state's natural environment. It was true that the state did not have the really bad air or water pollution of some US cities. There were other problems, though, such as the loss of natural tallgrass prairies and habitats for wildlife.

Iowans found ways to make changes. South of Des Moines, for example, local and state agencies pressured the federal government to establish the Neal Smith National Wildlife Refuge. More than 5,000 acres (2,023 ha) were set aside to restore prairie to what it looked like around 150 years ago. Thanks to these efforts, tall prairie grasses once again bend in the steady breeze, and many types of wildflower provide brilliant splashes of color. Small groups of wild buffalo have been reintroduced to the prairie, along with other animals and birds that

Prairie trillium is just one of the many different types of flowers growing in Iowa.

were once common prairie residents. The Prairie Learning Center gives visitors a chance to learn more about Iowa's prairies. As more farmland is purchased, the refuge continues to grow.

Other small wildlife preserves are scattered throughout Iowa, including several that form part of the Upper Mississippi River Wildlife and Fish Refuge. The Hayden Prairie State Reserve, near Chester, only covers 242 acres (98 ha), but it has around 100 different species of wildflower.

Northeastern Iowa has Red Cedar Woodland in Muscatine County. This preserve is a protected area that is part of a large island in the Cedar River. It can only be reached by boat, so the woodland is a perfect place for plants, such as maples and sycamores, and birds, such as bald eagles and hawks, to live and grow undisturbed.

In another part of the state, the people of Albia, Iowa, faced a different environmental problem. As coal mining became less popular in the region, many buildings were abandoned. Victorian buildings, which had once been elegant, had fallen into disrepair. They were covered with coal dust and grime. Some newspapers called Albia the "ugliest town in Iowa."

In 1970, Albians launched Operation Facelift. Buildings were restored and painted. Businesses were drawn to the area because of low rents and because there were so many skilled workers living in Albia. Within a decade, Albia became a model for restoring a community. In 1985, the efforts of Albia's residents were recognized. The entire downtown area, including more than ninety Victorian structures, was added to the National Register of Historic Places.

From the state's beautiful wildlife and natural scenery to its historic buildings, Iowans are dedicated to protecting the Hawkeye State.

Iowa has many programs and laws in place to protect the state's native animals. Residents of the state can also visit wildlife centers and sanctuaries to learn more about Iowa wildlife.

Plants & Animals

Sandhill Crane

When fully grown, these large, graceful birds can stand more than 3 feet (.9 m) tall. Cranes walk through shallow waters of rivers and lakes, feeding on small fish. The sandhill cranes migrate from Central America to nesting grounds as far north as Alaska. These beautiful birds are a frequent sight on the Iowa flyways.

Eastern Red Cedar

The Eastern red cedar grows in all parts of the state. In the wild, the trees provide homes for animals. People often plant these cedars to block the wind or to keep soil in certain areas from washing away. The wood is also used in furniture like closets or cabinets and for fence posts.

Muskrat

These large rodents are common in and around Iowa's lakes and ponds. Because of their brown fur and their heavy 12-inch (30.5 cm) tails, muskrats are often mistaken for beavers. Like beavers, muskrats spend much of their time in the water. Muskrat fur was prized by pioneer settlers.

Bald Eagle

In the past, the populations of bald eagles in Iowa—and across the country—were shrinking due to events such as pollution, overhunting, and habitat destruction. Laws and wildlife programs have helped to protect these majestic eagles, and, in 2007, they were taken off the list of endangered species. In Keokuk, at the southeastern tip of the state, shuttle buses take bird watchers to observation areas where they can see these magnificent birds.

Prairie Grasses

The western two-thirds of Iowa were once covered with a variety of grasses. Some of these grasses ranged in height between 1 foot and 7 feet (0.3–2 m). The prairie grasses provided homes and food for many different kinds of wildlife. In Iowa today, grasses such as little and big blue stem, Indian grass, Iowa barley, barnyard grass, blue grass, and bent grass grow on the prairies.

Elk

Millions of elk once roamed Iowa's prairies, eating grasses and other plants. Today, the Neal Smith National Wildlife Refuge maintains a herd of elk within a 700-acre (283 ha) enclosure. Elk are an important part of the prairie ecosystem. By grazing on larger prairie grasses, they allow smaller seedlings to get the sunlight and water they need to grow.

From the Beginning

The first humans moved into the region that now includes Iowa about 12,000 years ago, as the last of the giant glaciers retreated. These early native people lived by gathering wild foods and hunting.

About 3,000 years ago, the ancestors of modern Native Americans learned to grow crops. This provided a more reliable food supply and also allowed them to live in settled communities. They did not have to follow herds of wild animals or move south during the winter months to find wild plants and other sources of food.

Also around this time, there was another remarkable development. Early Native American people built large ceremonial mounds. Some of these mounds measured 130 feet (40 m) long and up to 70 feet (21 m) wide. The mounds were used for both burials and for religious ceremonies. Many mounds were built in the shape of animals such as birds and bears. A few of the mounds resembled human forms.

A young Iowan helps out at his family's store in Des Moines around 1940.

At one time, an estimated 10,000 of these mounds were spread through the middle of North America. The groups of people who built these mounds were part of the Hopewell Tradition. Ancient artifacts found in the mounds have been examined by scientists. They believe that the early people who lived in the area of Iowa may have traded with different natives living around the Rocky Mountains to the west, the Atlantic Coast in the east, along the Great Lakes to the north, and near the Gulf of Mexico in the south. As pioneer settlers cleared the land for farming, they destroyed all but about 200 of these mounds. Those that remain in Iowa are carefully protected, and only scientists are allowed to search the mounds.

Effigy Mounds National Monument, near Marquette, contains about 200 mounds. They were made of soil brought from the forest then mixed with clay from the riverbanks.

This painted woodcut gives an idea of what a Sioux village may have once looked like.

About 700 years ago, the Hopewell people vanished. No one knows for certain what happened to them. It is possible that they moved to other parts of the continent or were driven out by other groups of people. All that remains today are their amazing mounds.

In the years that followed, other native groups made their homes in the region. The Iowa (or Ioway) and the Omaha settled in the northwestern part of the state by the Big Sioux River. The Oto, the Missouri, the Sioux, the Illiniwek (or Illinois), and the Ottawa also lived and hunted in the land that includes present-day Iowa. Other groups also came to this area, including the Sauk and the Fox. The Fox were also called the Meskwaki or Mesquakie.

Native Americans provided food for their families by farming the land, hunting wild animals, and gathering wild foods. As farmers, they built villages and planted crops such as corn, beans, and squash. As hunters and gatherers, the natives traveled in the summer months on long hunting trips and lived in portable homes, such as tepees, as they searched for deer, elk, and bison.

There were, at one time, so many native groups living in the region that fights broke out over who could live there and who had the right to hunt. Other types of wars were fought among Native Americans because some groups were enemies of other groups. This caused some natives to be forced out of the area, usually moving farther west. The Iowa people were one of these groups.

Indian groups, or tribes, were often led by chiefs.

This illustration shows Jolliet and Marquette moving down the Mississippi with their Native American guides.

New Arrivals

In the 1600s, white settlers began to visit the region that now includes Iowa. Two of the first were the French explorers Louis Jolliet and Father Jacques Marquette, who traveled down the Mississippi River by canoe in 1673. Jolliet and Marquette were searching for a river passageway that traveled from the east to the Pacific Ocean in the west. They most likely did not stay for very long in the land that includes present-day Iowa. However, they did take note of some of the native cultures and the wildlife found on Iowa's shores of the Mississippi River.

In 1682, another French explorer called Sieur de La Salle traveled down the Mississippi. As La Salle traveled down the river, he claimed all the land—which stretched from Canada to the Gulf of Mexico—on both sides of the river for France. The land was called the Louisiana Territory, in honor of France's king, Louis XIV.

In the years that followed, fur traders from the French colonies in Canada also traveled through the region that would become Iowa. They traded with the different Native American groups that they came across, but they did not establish any permanent settlements. As more European explorers and settlers came to the area, they brought modern goods for the natives to use. The Native Americans traded for guns and the tame horses the Europeans brought with them.

During most of the 1700s, the French Canadians and the Native Americans got along well. For example, for many years the natives of the region had found ways to mine lead. French-Canadian traders, like Julien Dubuque, who were on good terms with the Natives also took part in the lead mining. In 1788, Dubuque began to establish a very profitable mining site and settlement. Besides providing lead, Dubuque's industry increased trade to the region, bringing in goods from the East and other places. The city of Dubuque is named for this early settler.

A New Country

In the late 1700s, another drama was occurring far to the east. Great Britain had earlier established thirteen colonies along the Atlantic coast of North America. By the late 1700s, there were nearly three million people living in those colonies. In 1776, the colonies declared their independence from the British. When the American Revolution ended in 1783, the colonies became the independent country of the United States of America.

In 1803, France agreed to sell the Louisiana Territory (which included the area that would later become Iowa) to the United States for about $15 million, which would be over $200 million in today's dollars. When the new government bought this land from France, the size of the United States nearly doubled. This land deal was called the Louisiana Purchase. Explorers Meriwether Lewis and William Clark worked for the US government, searching for a water route from the east to the west. Their explorations took them through the Louisiana Territory. Between 1804 and 1806, the Lewis and Clark Expedition explored the land that stretched from the Mississippi River, through present-day Iowa, and then even further toward the west, almost to the Pacific Ocean. Lewis and Clark

The Sergeant Floyd Memorial in Sioux City honors the only casualty of the Lewis and Clark Expedition.

The St. Paul and Sioux City R.R. Co.

ARE OFFERING THEIR

CHOICE LANDS in

South-western Minnesota and North-western Iowa,

at prices ranging from $4 to $6 per acre, on the most favorable terms.

These lands are acknowledged to be superior to any in the North-west, being in the great Wheat Belt, the crops of Corn, Sorghum, Flax, Hemp, Barley, Rye, and Oats, are very prolific.

No section of the N. W. offers lands so well adapted for STOCK RAISING and DAIRY purposes, being celebrated for its superior Grasses and well watered by Lakes and Streams. Climate unsurpassed. For Maps and Pamphlets giving full particulars, address

Land Department St. Paul & Sioux City R.R. Co., St. Paul, Minn.

Railroad companies often placed ads in newspapers. They hoped to attract settlers who were looking for new land.

would eventually extend their search to the West Coast, ending their travels at the Pacific coast of Oregon. As they explored these lands, they took note of the different types of animals and plants and the native cultures they encountered.

One of the most amazing aspects of the Lewis and Clark Expedition was their ability to survive hardship and danger. Fifty-six men traveled through the unmapped wilderness for nearly three years. During their travels, they encountered nearly thirty different Native American groups who spoke many different languages. They also faced bone-chilling weather conditions, rugged mountains, and losses of supplies. And yet only one man died during this expedition. Sergeant Charles Floyd died of problems caused by an inflamed appendix, a small organ attached to the gut. Floyd was buried near present-day Sioux City, and today a 100-foot-(30.5 m) tall monument marks his grave.

A Clash of Cultures

In the early 1800s, the United States began to grow and to expand with startling speed. Pioneer families pushed westward, hungry for the promise of land. They soon crossed the Mississippi River and started buying land from Native Americans when they could. When the Native American people were not willing to sell their land, the settlers often fought with them. In many cases, they forced the natives off of the land. Many of the Native Americans throughout the Midwest felt the pressure of the westward movement of settlers onto their land.

Iowa's first capitol bulding still stands on the campus of the University of Iowa, in Iowa City.

The Battle of Bad Axe, or Bad Axe Massacre, marked the end of the Black Hawk War. Hundreds of Sauk and Fox Indians were killed as they tried to cross the Mississippi River.

Some groups moved farther west to get away from the white settlers who were moving in from the east. In 1831, the US government ordered the Sauk and Fox Indians—who were then living in what would become Illinois—to move into the area that would become Iowa. Black Hawk, a Sauk chief, did not want to move his people. He wanted to reclaim his homeland. To do this, he brought together many warriors and organized an uprising in 1832. The conflict, called the Black Hawk War, ended in defeat for the Native Americans.

Because he lost this war, Chief Black Hawk agreed to give a strip of land 50 miles (80.5 km) wide along the Mississippi River to the US government. He hoped this land, known as the Black Hawk Purchase, would satisfy the settlers' hunger for land. Settlers rapidly moved to this land, and, in 1834, it became part of the Michigan Territory. Westward settlement by the whites continued.

Iowa Becomes a State

Before 1838, Iowa had been a part of the Wisconsin Territory. In 1838, the Iowa Territory was established. Robert Lucas was appointed as the first governor. In 1839, the territorial capital was built in Iowa City. The population continued to grow.

By 1846, more than 100,000 white settlers lived in Iowa. On December 28, 1846, Iowa was admitted to the Union as the 29th state. Iowa City was the state's capital. In 1857, however, the capital was moved to Des Moines. This was because Des Moines was closer to the center of the state.

In Their Own Words

Let us tackle the big issues with bold ideas that transform Iowa to accomplish our shared mission to grow Iowa and realize our shared vision of Iowa as the best place to live, work, and raise a family.

— Tom Vilsack, US Secretary of Agriculture and former Iowa governor

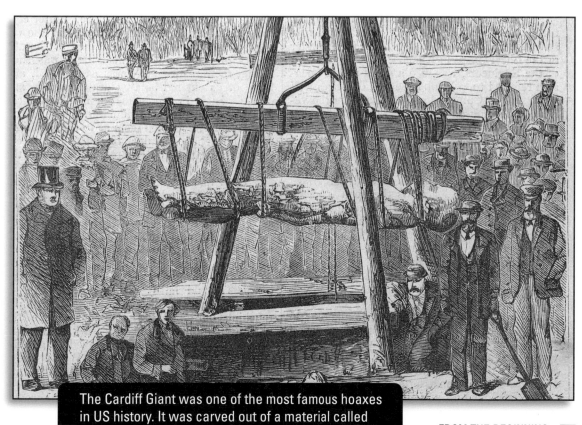

The Cardiff Giant was one of the most famous hoaxes in US history. It was carved out of a material called gypsum mined in Fort Dodge.

During the 1850s, Iowa continued to grow at a quick pace as word spread of the state's rich soil. Farmers knew that such good soil meant that crops would be successful and profitable. By 1860, more than 650,000 people lived in the state. Most of the settlers chose land in eastern Iowa and along river valleys in the western region of Iowa. They chose these locations because the forests in these areas provided plenty of wood for building homes, barns, and fences. The many rivers also provided transportation and waterpower for mills, which were used to grind corn and other grains. Settlers avoided the Great Plains area in the central and western regions of the state because the grassland had few trees and the land did not look like it could be farmed. The sod, or soil made up of centuries of matted, tangled grasses, seemed too thick for a plow to cut through. As a result, the settlers pressed rapidly across the grasslands, heading for fertile lands in Oregon and California.

Pioneer families in Iowa grew corn, wheat, and oats. Corn, which was used primarily to feed livestock, soon became the major crop. Farmers also raised cattle and hogs. Towns were established along the rivers because of the ease of transportation. Most of the state's cities, including Des Moines, Cedar Rapids, Davenport, Iowa City, and Dubuque, began this way.

The period from the 1840s to 1860 were Iowa's frontier days. Law and order were established slowly in some of the western towns. This made it a dangerous place to live, but many brave settlers pushed through and carved a life out of the land. This period also marked the late stages of the colorful steamboat days. These boats powered by steam traveled down the Mississippi and Missouri rivers, bringing goods, visitors, and new settlers.

These were also some of the last years for Native Americans living in Iowa. By 1851, all lands that had once belonged to Iowa's Native Americans became the property of the US government. In 1857, a band of Sioux warriors attacked a pioneer settlement at Spirit Lake, killing about forty people. The Native Americans were angry over the loss of their land and the way their culture was changing because of the settlers. The incident was called the Spirit Lake Massacre, and it was the last armed Native American resistance in Iowa. By 1860, very few Native Americans were left in the state.

In 1861, the fight between the Southern states, called the Confederacy, and the Northern states, called the Union, erupted into the Civil War. The main issue that started the war was slavery. Many people in the North did not believe it was right for any person to be a slave. However, many people in the South needed slaves in order to run their farms. The Southern states voted to secede, or separate, from the Union.

Iowans were deeply involved in the conflict over slavery. When Iowa was made into a state, it had been admitted as a Free State, which meant that it was a state in which slavery was not allowed. However, Missouri, which bordered Iowa to the south, was a slave state. Slaves in Missouri often tried to escape to Iowa. Many slaves were helped to freedom by Iowans who worked for the Underground

Steamboats moved people and cargo up and down the Mississippi River. Some boats even took part in races!

MAKING A CORNHUSK DOLL

A cornhusk doll was one of the many ways that Iowa's residents made use of corn. These dolls are still popular today and can be found at craft fairs throughout the state. Follow these instructions to make your own cornhusk doll.

WHAT YOU NEED

10-12 pieces of corn husk (you can use corn husks from fresh corn or buy dried husks from craft stores)
Several sheets of newspaper
Large bowl of tap water
Damp rag or towel
Scissors
6-8 cotton balls
Light twine or strong thread
Ruler
Pipe cleaner or flexible wire
Craft glue
Corn silk or scraps of yarn
Black and red markers

If the corn husks are green, allow them to dry for a few days between sheets of newspaper. When the husks are a light tan color, soak them in water for about 5 minutes. This will make them easier to shape.

Spread newspaper on your work surface. Keep husks you are not ready to use under a damp towel. You can cut off pointed ends to make the husks more even.

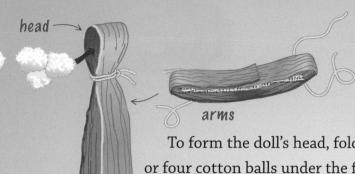

head

arms

To form the doll's head, fold a large piece of husk in half. Stuff three or four cotton balls under the fold. About 1.5 inches (4 cm) from the fold, tie a piece of twine to create the neck. The ends of the husk should reach several inches below the neck.

To make the arms, wrap a thin piece of husk around a 6-inch-(15 cm) piece of pipe cleaner or wire. The husk should be about 1 inch (2.5 cm) longer than the pipe cleaner. Fold back the ends of the husk at each end of the wire and tie them to form wrists. Slide the arms between the two pieces of husk below the head. When you are finished with the doll, the arms can be carefully bent into many different positions.

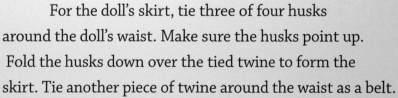

Stuff four or five cotton balls below the arms to fill out the body, then tie a piece of twine to create the waist.

tie

fold down

For the doll's skirt, tie three of four husks around the doll's waist. Make sure the husks point up. Fold the husks down over the tied twine to form the skirt. Tie another piece of twine around the waist as a belt.

Glue corn silk or yarn to give the doll hair. Use the markers to draw a face. Give your doll as a gift or display it at home.

Railroad. This was a secret network of people who hid runaway slaves and guided them to the Northern states or to Canada.

Iowans helped in other ways, too. During the Civil War, more than 80,000 Iowans served in the Union army. This was a higher percentage of the population than in any other state. Though many Iowa soldiers died or were wounded in battle, no battles were fought on Iowa land. The Civil War ended in 1865, and the Southern states rejoined the Union.

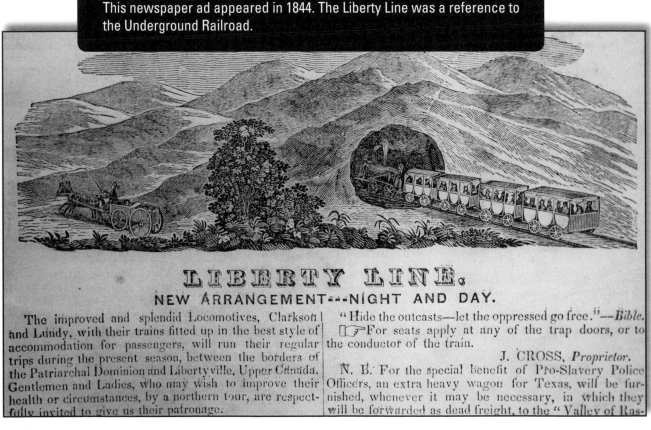

This newspaper ad appeared in 1844. The Liberty Line was a reference to the Underground Railroad.

LIBERTY LINE.
NEW ARRANGEMENT---NIGHT AND DAY.

The improved and splendid Locomotives, Clarkson and Lundy, with their trains fitted up in the best style of accommodation for passengers, will run their regular trips during the present season, between the borders of the Patriarchal Dominion and Libertyville, Upper Canada. Gentlemen and Ladies, who may wish to improve their health or circumstances, by a northern tour, are respectfully invited to give us their patronage.

"Hide the outcasts—let the oppressed go free."—*Bible*.
☞For seats apply at any of the trap doors, or to the conductor of the train.

J. CROSS, *Proprietor*.

N. B. For the special benefit of Pro-Slavery Police Officers, an extra heavy wagon for Texas, will be furnished, whenever it may be necessary, in which they will be forwarded as dead freight, to the "Valley of Ras-

Pioneers defend their land claim in Guthrie in the late 1880s.

A Century of Growth and Change

After the Civil War, several changes opened Iowa's prairie lands to farming. Harder steel blades were made, so farmers could put them on their plows and easily cut through the sod. In addition, swamps were drained to create even more farmland. By draining the swamps, though, farmers were contributing to long droughts that were a problem for Midwestern agriculture throughout the 1900s. It would not be until the late twentieth century that people found that these wetlands were essential to keeping the environment in balance.

The invention of barbed wire made it possible to build fences around fields without using much wood. This was ideal for the plains and prairies since not much wood was available. Houses were made out of sod instead of wood. The thick sod was cut into large cubes and then stacked like blocks. Wood was needed only for framing doors, windows, and a roof. The whole structure could be built for only about thirty dollars.

JOHN DEERE TRACTOR COMPANY
WATERLOO, IOWA

At first, most of Iowa's major manufacturing industries were related to agriculture, such as the John Deere Tractor Company in Waterloo.

The railroad also helped prairie settlement. By 1880, more than 5,000 miles (8,047 km) of track crisscrossed the state. This meant that almost every farm was within 25 miles (40 km) of the railroad. Railroad companies brought thousands of immigrants directly from European and Asian countries to Iowa. These workers cleared the land and laid down the tracks. Some moved west when they were done, but others settled in Iowa. By 1900, all of the state's land was claimed.

In the early 1900s, Iowa became the country's leading producer of corn and hogs. The fertile soil and good climate allowed Iowans to increase agricultural production year after year. Sometimes the farm surpluses, or food that the farmers did not need to feed their families and their animals, were so great that the prices for these products fell. In other words, there was more food than anyone needed to buy. In order to sell it, farmers had to keep lowering their prices. This was bad for farmers since they could not make a lot of money to continue to support their farms.

In order to try to stop this from happening again, Iowans tried to grow different kinds of crops, instead of having everyone grow the same things. These efforts to change were only partly successful, though. Soybeans from China were tried by some farmers in 1910, but they did not become a major crop until later in the century.

Industry also became more important after 1900. Many of the manufacturing establishments were related to farming, including railroad cars and tractors. Factories were established in or near the cities, offering jobs to people who did not want to farm. This, in turn, increased city populations. Today all of the state's cities and large towns have some kind of industry.

Still, the state's prosperity rose and fell on the profits made mostly from agricultural products like corn and hogs. Around 1917, during World War I, the armies of the United States and its allies (England and France) needed large amounts of food. Along with other states, Iowa's farmers did their best to supply it. During these years, Iowa's farms set new production records. This did not last very long, though. In the years that followed the war, Iowa's overproduction led to sagging prices again. There was so much food, farmers had to reduce their prices again.

The Great Depression started in 1929, and it brought with it hard times for millions of Americans. Businesses and banks closed, and millions of people lost their jobs. Without work, many could not afford their homes. Farms in many states, including Iowa, were abandoned because the farmers and their families did not have enough money to continue working the farms. Even if they did, most Americans at the time did not have a lot of money and could not buy the products. Severe droughts added to the problems of farm families. Crops were lost because of the lack of rain. Many Iowans moved west in search of new opportunities.

The US government established some programs that tried to help Americans during the Great Depression. One of these programs created jobs that improved the country. Many men were sent to different states to build roads and bridges. Others were sent to the forests to work in the lumber industry. World War II also helped the economy. Although many lives were lost during this war, the need for supplies helped to pull the country out of the Great Depression. Iowa farms and factories again provided supplies for the troops.

After the war, many Iowans started moving away from the farmland and into the cities and large towns. They did this to look for jobs with more stable incomes than farming provided. By 1960, for the first time, more than half of the state's people lived in urban areas. They had grown tired of the farm economy that continued to ride the roller coaster of changing prices and profits. Some Iowans gave up on agriculture completely and moved away from the state. During the 1970s and 1980s, Iowa's population decreased by more than 150,000. Entire towns were abandoned.

However, the state experienced a heartening comeback beginning in the 1990s. Many communities began to encourage new businesses to come to Iowa. The skilled workers living in the Hawkeye State were one of the reasons why businesses moved to Iowa. The state is home to several colleges and universities. Not only do these schools produce skilled and educated professionals, but they also attract newcomers to the state. The tourism industry has also improved, and many people come to experience Iowa's frontier history and culture. Farmers have been growing a variety of crops, including soybeans, which make the state an important agricultural producer for the world market.

Iowa's unique system of voting in a primary election, called a caucus, makes it an important state for presidential candidates.

Important Dates

★ **8,500 BC** The first people arrive in what will become Iowa.

★ **300 to 1450** Ancient people called Mound Builders live in the region.

★ **1673** Jolliet and Marquette become the first Europeans to reach present-day Iowa.

★ **1682** French Explorer Sieur de La Salle claims the Mississippi River region.

★ **1788** Julien Dubuque starts the first European settlement in present-day Iowa.

★ **1803** The US government gains the land that includes Iowa as part of the Louisiana Purchase.

★ **1832** The Black Hawk War is fought, and Sauk and Fox warriors are defeated by the US Army.

★ **1838** Congress creates the Iowa Territory.

★ **1846** On December 28, Iowa becomes the 29th state.

★ **1857** Des Moines becomes the state capital.

★ **1867** The first railroad across Iowa is completed.

★ **1917 to 1918** More than 100,000 Iowans serve in World War I.

★ **1920s to 1930s** Low crop prices cause thousands of families to lose their land.

★ **1929 to 1933** Iowan Herbert Hoover serves as president of the United States.

★ **1930s to 1940s** Nearly 200,000 Iowans serve in World War II.

★ **1960s** More Iowans live in urban areas than in rural areas.

★ **1989** An airplane crash at Sioux City claims 111 lives.

★ **1993** Flooding due to heavy rains causes more than $2 billion in damages.

★ **1999** Governor Terry Branstad—who served as Iowa's governor for 16 years—holds the record for the most years as Iowa's governor.

★ **2005** The Iowa Events Center in Des Moines opens, featuring four different entertainment and convention complexes.

★ **2008** Cedar Rapids, Iowa City, and other areas experience devastating floods lasting nearly a month and causing billions of dollars in damages.

The People

Ninety percent of Iowa is farmland. Over ninety percent of Iowa's population is made up of white people who trace their ancestry to Europe. However, that does not mean Iowa is made up of only white farmers. The Hawkeye State has a rich cultural history and a diverse population. Many residents are the descendants of settlers who came to Iowa from countries in Europe, Asia, South America, and Africa. Iowa is also home to many different religious communities.

Native Iowa

Before white settlers came to the region, the only people living on the land that would become Iowa were Native Americans. In the years following the Black Hawk War, though, most Native American groups moved out of Iowa. After the Spirit Lake Massacre in 1857, nearly all of the remaining Native Americans were driven out of the state. In that same year, however, a small band of Meskwaki and Sauk came back into Iowa and purchased about 80 acres (32 ha) of prairie farmland.

> ## In Their Own Words
>
> *Iowa is home to teachers, farmers, lawyers, factory workers, and many others who work hard every day to provide the best for their families and their future.*
>
> — Leonard Boswell, former US Congressman from Iowa

Some Iowans live in and around the cities, while others prefer life in farming communities such as Garden City.

Powwows in Iowa celebrate the history and culture of many Native American groups.

Population of Iowa in 2010

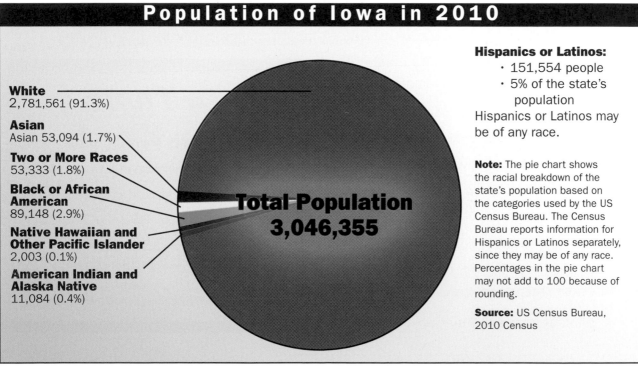

White
2,781,561 (91.3%)

Asian
Asian 53,094 (1.7%)

Two or More Races
53,333 (1.8%)

Black or African American
89,148 (2.9%)

Native Hawaiian and Other Pacific Islander
2,003 (0.1%)

American Indian and Alaska Native
11,084 (0.4%)

Total Population 3,046,355

Hispanics or Latinos:
· 151,554 people
· 5% of the state's population
Hispanics or Latinos may be of any race.

Note: The pie chart shows the racial breakdown of the state's population based on the categories used by the US Census Bureau. The Census Bureau reports information for Hispanics or Latinos separately, since they may be of any race. Percentages in the pie chart may not add to 100 because of rounding.

Source: US Census Bureau, 2010 Census

During World War II, residents from all parts of Iowa defended the United States. These Meskwaki men trained at a Marshalltown facility before fighting in the war.

Over the years, the Meskwaki bought more land. Today, the Meskwaki settlement covers nearly 3,500 acres (1,416 ha) of farmland in a fertile river valley in Tama County. This is the only Native American settlement in the state. The Meskwaki are especially proud of the fact that this is land that they purchased and own. In other states, many Native American settlements are on reservations. Reservation land was set aside for Native Americans by the US government, and, in many cases, the natives were forced to live there after their traditional lands were taken away.

The Meskwaki hold a four-day powwow every year in August. This event was originally a religious and social celebration of the corn harvest. By the early 1900s, however, more and more non-natives came to watch the ceremonies. Today, the traditional dances remain the major part of the Meskwaki Powwow, but the foods, crafts, and costumes are also popular. It is a great opportunity for people to learn about Native American history and culture in Iowa.

The Meskwaki are not the only Native Americans in Iowa. Many Native American Iowans live in cities and towns, working in a variety of industries. Some live on farms in rural areas. Though Native Americans make up less than 1 percent of the population, they are still important to the state.

Diversity

As more of Iowa was opened up for farming, and as the cities and towns developed in the 1800s, thousands of immigrants came directly from different northern European countries, including the Netherlands, Norway, Sweden, and Denmark. Small numbers came from southern Europe as well, such as the Italians and Croatians who came to work in the coalfields of southern Iowa.

These newcomers often settled near people who were from the same part of Europe. This gave them the comfort of sharing a familiar language and customs. In 1847, for example, immigrants from the Netherlands founded the town of Pella. They constructed buildings similar to buildings in their European homeland. This includes a windmill in the town square. Every spring, the people of Pella hold a festival called Tulip Time, featuring costumes, food, crafts, and dances from the nineteenth century.

Other ethnic communities celebrate their heritage in similar ways. The large Irish-American community in Emmetsburg has a special Saint Patrick's Day Celebration every March. Other annual celebrations include a Danish festival in Elk Horn, called Tivoli Fest, a Nordic festival in Decorah, and a Swedish Santa Lucia Festival in Stanton during the Christmas season.

In the 1850s, a community was built in Buxton, with houses on even plots of land. Freed blacks were offered the chance to live here, and for a time it was a model community for African Americans. The town's population of more than 5,000 was nearly 60 percent African American. The rest of the population included Swedish, Italian, and Croatian immigrants. For more than thirty years, beginning around 1880, Buxton's people all got along well. There were few signs of racial tension between people of different ethnic backgrounds. African Americans called it "the black man's utopia." (A utopia is a perfect place where everyone can be happy.) When the economy faltered late in the 1920s and 1930s, though, people of all backgrounds began to leave the state. Today only about 3 percent of the state's population is African American, and they live primarily in urban areas, including Des Moines and Waterloo.

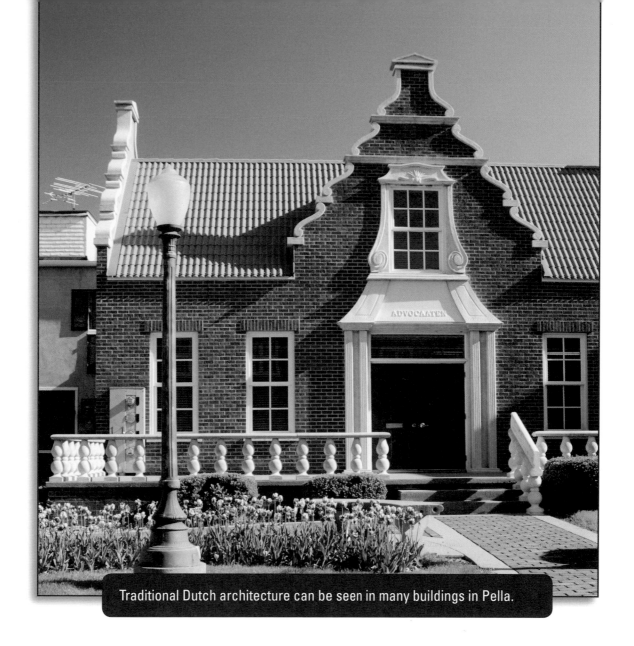

Traditional Dutch architecture can be seen in many buildings in Pella.

Iowa's Hispanic population accounts for about 5 percent of the population. They represent the largest ethnic minority in the state. Some Hispanic Iowans have lived in the state for many generations. Many others are recent immigrants from Mexico and Central American countries. Job opportunities in the cities and on farms are some of the reasons that Hispanics and many others move to Iowa.

Famous Iowans

Herbert Hoover: US President

In 1874, Herbert Hoover was born in a village in Iowa. Hoover was trained as an engineer, and he and his wife traveled around the world to different countries. Hoover always showed great concern for people who were suffering. He organized relief efforts that saved hundreds of thousands of people from starvation in different parts of the world. Herbert Hoover served as US secretary of commerce in the 1920s, was elected president in 1928, and served until 1933. He died in 1964.

Cloris Leachman: Actress

Cloris Leachman was born in Des Moines in 1926. She made her television debut in 1948. Through the years, Leachman has performed in plays and musicals on stage. She is well known for her roles on television and in the movies, and she has won an Academy Award and several Emmy Awards.

Kurt Warner: NFL Quarterback

Kurt Warner was born in Burlington in 1971. He played high school football in Cedar Rapids and college football at the University of Northern Iowa. Warner made his NFL debut in 1998 with the St. Louis Rams. He twice led his team to the Super Bowl and won in 2000.

Ashton Kutcher: Actor and Producer

Christopher Ashton Kutcher was born in Cedar Rapids in 1978. He left college to work as a model and was soon cast in the hit television show, *That '70s Show*. He has appeared in many feature films and has produced television shows and movies, too.

John Wayne: Actor

Marion Morrison, better known as John Wayne, was born in Winterset in 1907. He starred in more than 200 films, usually as the strong, slow-speaking Western hero, and became one of Hollywood's most popular actors. He won an Academy Award for his role in *True Grit*. John Wayne died in 1979.

Carrie Chapman Catt: Feminist and Suffragist

Carrie Chapman Catt was born in Wisconsin in 1859, but grew up in Charles City, Iowa. Catt was one of the leading figures in the struggle for woman's suffrage—the right to vote. She helped convince the US Congress to pass the Nineteenth Amendment, which granted women the right to vote, in time for women to vote in the 1920 presidential election. Catt also fought for other rights for women. She died in 1947.

Quick Facts

Grant Wood, an American artist, was born and raised in Iowa. His most famous painting is called *American Gothic*. The house that inspired the painting is in the town of Eldon and now belongs to the State Historical Society of Iowa.

Religious Communities

Several religious groups were drawn to the fertile Iowa farmland in the 1800s. Some of the most famous of these religious communities in Iowa are the seven Amana Colonies located southwest of present-day Cedar Rapids. This religious group began in Germany in the 1700s, but their beliefs were unpopular with established churches. They moved to New York in 1842 and then came to Iowa. The Amana Colonies are located on scenic hilly land where they used to live a communal lifestyle in which the people all shared the land and all their resources. Although the colonies and people are still there, the traditions and ways of life for the residents have changed and become more modern. The seven closely knit communities are a major tourist attraction, drawing thousands of tourists every year. The communities are famous for their German-style restaurants and handcrafted woodwork. The Amana Oktoberfest is one of the state's most popular festivals, offering a rich sampling of German foods and drinks, as well as costumes, dances, and crafts.

Another religious group, the Amish, established settlements in southeastern Iowa. As in other Amish communities throughout the United States, the Amish people in Iowa follow simple, eighteenth-century ways of living, avoiding most modern machinery. They even drive horse-drawn carriages instead of cars.

The Mormons—members of the Church of Jesus Christ of Latter-day Saints—also set up communities in Iowa. In the 1840s, a large group of Mormons from Illinois moved west and eventually settled in the region that later became Utah. A large group of Mormons decided to stay in Iowa and purchased land in the southern part of the state around Lamoni. They remained there from 1846 to 1852, and then joined the larger Mormon community in Utah. There are still Mormons living throughout Iowa, though there are no distinct Mormon-only communities.

Education in Iowa

Iowans are proud of the state's long tradition of excellence in education. That tradition began in 1830, when the state's first school was opened. Today, nearly all adult Iowans are literate, or able to read and write. In fact, more than 90 percent of the state's people have completed high school, which is one of the highest rates in the nation.

The state also has outstanding colleges and universities. The University of Iowa, founded in 1847, has its major campus in Iowa City. The university is well

Both academics and athletics are important parts of student life at the University of Iowa.

Many Iowa cities, such as Dubuque, are a mixture of historic small-town charm and modern urban development. This is just one of the many reasons why Iowans love their state.

known for its programs in the fine arts. The university's Writer's Workshop is famous around the world. The state's most famous artist, Grant Wood, did much of his work at the university, too.

Iowa State University of Science and Technology, founded in Ames in 1858, was one of the first schools to offer college courses on agricultural science. It is also a leader in veterinary medicine. Both Iowa State University and the University of Iowa are well known for their sports programs, especially football and basketball. The University of Iowa is considered to have the top wrestling program in the country, a program that has produced many national champions and Olympic medalists.

Living in Iowa

While Iowa does have several cities, none of them are large compared to many other US cities. Only Des Moines has more than 200,000 people. In fact, the ten largest Iowa cities combined total under 900,000 people. The low population density and lack of large cities help Iowa have some of the lowest crime rates in the country.

The lack of large cities also adds to the impression of Iowa as an example of small-town America. Nearly half the people do live in small towns or on farms. In the past, as settlers moved into Iowa, they purchased their land in what was called quarter sections of 160 acres (65 ha). This created a grid pattern of settlements, much like graph paper or a checkerboard. Today, many property lines in Iowa are still broken up this way.

Small-town architecture with traditional-looking buildings, such as Victorian homes, also reinforces the sense of small-town America. Pride in this nineteenth-century heritage is shown in the many festivals celebrating Iowa's pioneer days, including re-creations of sod houses, nineteenth-century farms, and river steamboats.

Although more than 90 percent of Iowa's land area is covered by farmland, Iowans enjoy a lively assortment of cultural opportunities, such as performances by musicians, dancers, and other artists. However, because the population is widely spread out, Iowans often rely on touring groups, or artists who travel from one town to another, for plays, dance performances, and concerts. The universities also serve as cultural centers. Besides offering performances, they also provide training in film, television, dance, and theater.

With its small-town charm, good schools, rich cultural history, fertile farmland, and thriving cities and towns, Iowa has a lot to offer its residents and visitors.

Calendar of Events

★ **St. Patrick's Day Celebration in Emmetsburg**

For a full three days in March, Emmetsburg celebrates St. Patrick's Day. Festivities include a Miss Shamrock Pageant, a marathon race, Irish dances, and a wide variety of food and entertainment.

★ **Tulip Festivals**

May is a month in which the state celebrates this European flower. A Tulip Festival is held in Orange City and Tulip Time is in Pella. Both celebrations honor the communities' Dutch heritage.

★ **Burlington Steamboat Days American Music Festival**

The town of Burlington has held this summer festival since 1963. This six-day event features music performances, a parade, a golf tournament, and a talent show.

★ **RAGBRAI**

Each summer thousands of cyclists bike across Iowa in the *Register*'s Annual Great Bicycle Race. The non-competitive race is often considered "part race, part parade, and part party."

★ **Midwest Old Threshers Reunion**

This event draws more than 100,000 visitors to Mount Pleasant on Labor Day weekend. A thresher is a type of farm equipment used on crops. This reunion includes demonstrations of nineteenth-century farm machinery and harvesting techniques.

★ Meskwaki Powwow

This August celebration, held in Tama, provides an opportunity for people to learn about and experience Native American culture. The powwow has displays of crafts, traditional clothing, food, and dances.

★ The National Balloon Classic in Indianola

Held in midsummer, this is one of the greatest hot-air balloon displays in the country. More than 100 hot-air balloons take to the sky during this three-day event. Visitors get to see the various balloons and can even take a ride in one!

★ Iowa State Fair

This Des Moines event is one of the oldest state fairs in the country and the largest event in Iowa. The first Iowa State Fair was held in 1854. The fair has been held at its present location since 1886! More than a million visitors come each year to tour some of the eighty buildings or to watch 16,000 entrants compete for prizes in cooking, canning, hog raising, and a wide variety of crafts and farm activities.

★ Iowa's Latino Heritage Festival

Though Iowa's Latino population is smaller than in some other states, this celebration of Latino heritage is the largest cultural event in the state. The festival features music, crafts, and traditional dances from Brazil, Mexico, and Puerto Rico.

How the Government Works

As in all states, there are different levels of government in Iowa. Different officials are responsible for a variety of duties. However, the one thing that is true at all levels: Iowa government is for Iowans. Iowa citizens elect their officials and the officials work toward addressing Iowans' needs and concerns.

Iowa's cities and towns are grouped together by location to form counties. Iowa is divided into ninety-nine counties, and each of them is governed by a three-member board of supervisors. Elections for these positions take place every four years. The county government collects city, school, county, and state taxes. The supervisors are responsible for local streets and roads, and they supervise the work of the sheriff's department, the county treasurer, the county attorney, and the courts.

Each town and city in Iowa also has its own government. Cities in Iowa are governed in two different ways. In some areas, an elected city council makes the laws that the cities will follow. In other places, a mayor or city manager acts as the executive of the city. Responsibilities for cities and towns include supervising city agencies such as police and fire departments.

President Obama campaigned in Des Moines the night before the 2012 presidential election.

Higher Levels of Government

Like most other states, Iowa has a state government that is broken up into three branches: executive, legislative, and judicial. These branches work together to make the laws and to make sure that the laws are being followed.

Iowa is also represented in the federal government through the US Congress. Iowa has two senators serving in the Senate and four representatives in the House of Representatives. All of these Iowan officials work to represent the Hawkeye State in national issues that affect Iowa.

From Bill to Law

When a new law is proposed at the state level of government, it is first called a bill. The ideas for bills often come from Iowa residents who have spoken to their representatives. Either a senator or a representative can introduce a bill into the General Assembly. If a senator proposed the bill, then the bill is first discussed in the senate. The bill is sent to a committee, which will examine it. The committee may hold hearings on this particular bill and invite expert opinions from people who are familiar with the subject. Interested citizens and officials of towns and

Branches of Government

EXECUTIVE ★ ★ ★ ★ ★ ★ ★ ★

The governor is the state's highest official. He or she is elected to a four-year term. The governor appoints the officers of about twenty state departments and agencies. Other top-level executive officers are also elected, including the lieutenant governor, secretary of state, auditor, treasurer, secretary of agriculture, and attorney general. The governor is responsible for seeing that laws are carried out. He or she also approves or rejects laws.

LEGISLATIVE ★ ★ ★ ★ ★ ★ ★ ★

The legislature, called the General Assembly, is made up of two houses. The senate has fifty members and the house of representatives has one hundred members. Committees in both houses hold hearings to consider changes in the law or new laws. Both houses need to approve laws before they are made official.

JUDICIAL ★ ★ ★ ★ ★ ★ ★ ★

The Iowa Supreme Court, with nine justices, is the highest court in the state. It reviews cases from lower courts, including the court of appeals and eight district courts. The justices of the Supreme Court help to interpret, or explain, the laws of the state. Lower courts try criminal cases, when a crime has been committed, and civil cases, which usually involve people who are suing others for money.

counties who are affected by the proposed law can ask to testify or speak. These people offer their reasons why they either want the bill to pass or why they believe the bill should be rejected. Senators vote on the bill, and if it passes, it is sent to the house of representatives. There, it goes through the same review process.

Once the bill has been approved by both houses, the governor signs it, and the bill becomes a law. If the governor does not agree with the bill, he or she can veto it. The bill can still pass if the General Assembly overrides the governor's veto. This happens if two-thirds of the members of each house votes in favor of the bill.

Making a Living

Although much of Iowa's land surface is devoted to agriculture, most Iowans are not farmers. Instead, Iowans work in a wide variety of occupations.

Agriculture

Farming, of course, is a major part of the state's economy. There are about 92,000 farms in the state, and the average farm covers about 333 acres (135 ha).

Prairie grasses that once grew up to 9 feet (2.7 m) tall have been replaced by corn and other crops. No state produces more corn than Iowa. In fact, about 20 percent of the nation's corn crops grow in Iowa. Most of the corn is used to feed livestock, including green corn stored in silos for winter feed. Corn is also used for cereal. One of the country's largest cereal plants is located in Cedar Rapids. Iowa is also a leader in producing corn oil, corn syrup, and popcorn. The country's largest popcorn processing plant is in Sioux City.

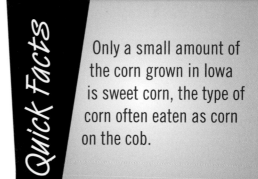

Quick Facts

Only a small amount of the corn grown in Iowa is sweet corn, the type of corn often eaten as corn on the cob.

A family of Iowans works together on their farm.

Iowa's Industries and Workers (April 2013)

Industry	Number of People Working in That Industry	Percentage of Labor Force Working in That Industry
Farming	52,400	3.3%
Mining and Logging	2,200	0.1%
Construction	62,500	4%
Manufacturing	216,800	13.8%
Trade, Transportation, and Utilities	308,200	19.6%
Information	25,900	1.6%
Financial Activities	104,100	6.6%
Professional and Business Services	129,700	8.3%
Education and Health Services	223,800	14.2%
Leisure and Hospitality	135,400	8.6%
Other Services	56,500	3.6%
Government	253,500	16.1%
Totals	**1,571,000**	**99.8%**

Notes: Figures above do not include people in the armed forces.
"Professionals" includes people such as doctors and lawyers.

Source: U.S. Bureau of Labor Statistics

Dairy farms throughout Iowa provide milk products for use in the state and around the country.

Iowa is also a major dairy state, with picturesque dairy farms dotting the hills of northeastern Iowa. Farms in all parts of the state also produce eggs and chickens, and some specialize in raising turkeys, sheep, and horses.

By far, the most important farm animals are hogs. Iowa has a hog population of more than 20 million. Hogs are one of the major sources of farm income, and no state raises more than Iowa. The Hawkeye State is also a leader in raising beef cattle. Beef herds graze the grasslands of southern and western Iowa. Some Iowa farmers buy cattle from western states and then fatten them in Iowa on corn.

In Iowa, soybeans are another major crop. Soybeans are used for cattle feed, but they are also used to make oil, soy milk, and tofu products. Iowa farmers also grow wheat, oats, hay, alfalfa, flax, and rye. The state's chief fruit crop is apples. In addition, many farm families grow a variety of table vegetables, including sweet corn, potatoes, green beans, onions, and tomatoes.

RECIPE FOR APPLE CRACKERS

The Delicious apple, one of the most popular apples in the nation, was developed in Iowa in the 1880s. Here is a quick and easy snack you can make with a couple of Red Delicious or Golden Delicious apples.

WHAT YOU NEED

2 Red Delicious or Golden Delicious apples

1 lemon

1/2 cup peanut butter or almond butter

1/4 cup raisins

6 to 8 graham crackers

honey

Have an adult help you peel, core, and slice the apples. Place the apple slices on a microwaveable plate in one layer. Then cut the lemon into quarter slices, remove the seeds, and squeeze each lemon piece over the apples. The lemon juice should coat the apple slices.

Place a sheet of wax paper over the top of the plate of apple slices. Set your microwave to high, place the plate of apples inside, and cook the apples for 2 to 3 minutes.

While you are waiting for the apples to cook, stir the raisins into the peanut or almond butter. If the mixture is too stiff, you can add a little honey to it. Then spread the nut butter mix on six to eight graham crackers.

When the apples are done cooking, let them cool for two or three minutes. Then place a few apple slices on each graham cracker. You can top off each cracker with a sprinkle of cinnamon, chocolate sprinkles, or coconut. Enjoy the tasty snack!

Iowa's fertile soil and available water are ideal for farming. Oddly enough, the most serious farm problem arises when all the farms have a great year. This surplus harvest—or having too much of certain crops—pushes prices down, which is bad for the farmers. In some years, farmers cannot sell all that they have grown. Since the 1930s, the federal government has offered some forms of help to farmers. At times, the government has even paid farmers to take some land out of production. In other words, the government pays them not to grow as many crops.

On a farm in Madison County, corn is stored in these bins before it is used to make products such as livestock feed.

Iowa steel mills, such as this one in Davenport, prepare steel to be used for a variety of products.

Manufacturing and Mining

Industries are an important source of jobs for Iowans. Food processing is the leading manufacturing activity. A number of cities have major meatpacking plants. Canned ham and breakfast sausage are popular products. Factories that process dairy products are scattered throughout the state. In addition, a number of industries manufacture tractors and other farm machinery.

There are a few companies involved in other kinds of manufacturing, too. Electrical equipment, especially household appliances, is important in several cities. Amana is a manufacturer of high-quality refrigerators. Winnebago Industries, headquartered in Forest City, produces motor homes.

Mining no longer plays a major role in Iowa's economy. In the past, coal mines were important, but most of the coal in Iowa has been dug out. Other mineral resources in Iowa include limestone, gypsum, clays, and gravel.

Services

Since the 1970s, the United States, including Iowa, has seen a steady decline in manufacturing. More manufacturing industries have been moved to other countries where labor costs are lower. In addition, many factory jobs once performed by people have been taken over by machines. As manufacturing has declined, the country's economy has become more involved with the service industry. This includes any job that performs a service, such as those involved with health, sales, hotels and restaurants, schools, and banks. By the early twenty-first century, services made up the largest portion of Iowa's economy, as they did in other states.

The largest service businesses are wholesale and retail sales. For example, a truck loaded with new cars that are delivered to a car dealership is engaged in wholesale trade. One owner of a business (the one making the cars) sells a product to another business owner (the car dealership). Then, when a car salesperson sells a vehicle to a customer, they are making a retail trade.

Transportation is an important service industry in Iowa. The state's rivers are ideal for transporting grains and other products.

Iowa's festivals, museums, and beautiful landscapes bring many tourists to the state each year.

In this case, a business is selling a product directly to a customer. The largest wholesale businesses in Iowa are those that sell tractors, farm machines, and cars to dealers. Other wholesale business involves the distribution of farm products to food processing plants. The state's leading retail businesses include restaurants and grocery stores.

Other service businesses include banking, real estate, and insurance. Banks in Des Moines, Davenport, and Sioux City provide services to businesses throughout the state. Several of the country's largest insurance companies have their headquarters in Des Moines.

Iowans also work in a variety of community and personal services, such as law offices, health-care facilities, and consulting businesses. Other kinds of service workers are paid by the government, including public school teachers and workers in state, county, and local government agencies.

Transportation and communication make up other service areas. Railroads, for example, have been important to Iowa farms and towns since the 1850s. Today, although there is not much passenger service, twenty railroad companies continue to carry freight throughout the state. In addition, river barges are still important for shipping bulk items such as grain. Iowa is the only state that has two navigable rivers—rivers that can be easily traveled down—on its borders.

In the field of communications, Iowa has more than 300 newspapers, with about 40 of them publishing daily. The *Des Moines Register* is considered one of the best newspapers in the nation. There are also magazines and other periodicals published in the state. In addition, Iowa has many radio stations and about forty television stations.

Tourism

Tourism has become increasingly important to the state in the past few decades. Iowa has a colorful history, and more and more visitors are drawn to its historical attractions such as the Living History Farms, west of Des Moines. This is an agricultural museum spread out over 500 acres (202 ha). The living demonstrations include re-creations of an Iowan Native American village from 1700, an 1850 pioneer farm, an 1875 village, and a 1900 horse-powered farm. Interpreters in costumes use authentic tools to show changes in farm life and agricultural technology through the years.

In a similar way, the town of Fort Dodge has drawn thousands of visitors with its Fort Museum and Frontier Town. This complete frontier village is considered one of the best pioneer museums in the country. Iowa also has a popular maritime museum, the Iowa Great Lakes Maritime Museum, in Arnolds Park. It includes the *Queen II*, a reproduction of the 1884 *Queen*, a paddle-wheel boat that traveled across the Great Lakes for about ninety years.

Iowans have also taken advantage of two popular films. A 1989 movie, *Field of Dreams*, featured a baseball field in the middle of an Iowa cornfield. The diamond made for the film still draws thousands of visitors from every state and from several countries. Another film, *The Bridges of Madison County*, has added to the number of tourists who come to see Iowa's famous covered bridges.

The National Mississippi River Museum & Aquarium in Dubuque, one of the largest river museums in the country, highlights the history of rafting and steamboating on the great river.

Products & Resources

Topsoil

Few places on Earth have been blessed with such deep, fertile soil. When pioneer farmers finally had steel plows that could cut through the thick prairie sod, they found rich, dark soil that was ideal for growing crops. The soil, along with Iowa's water and good transportation, have made the state a major part of America's "breadbasket," a good place to grow grains.

Tourism

Tourism is Iowa's fastest growing industry. Over the past several decades, residents have discovered that visitors are fascinated by Iowa's history and culture. Communities have spruced up Victorian-era houses and other old buildings, and have opened dozens of historic sites for tours.

Hogs

In the mid-1800s, the arrival of the railroads made it natural for Iowa farmers to raise beef cattle and hogs for profit. The animals could be raised on Iowa corn, then shipped by rail to meatpacking plants in Chicago. Today, there are five times as many hogs as people in Iowa! One-quarter of all the hogs in the United States are raised in Iowa.

Soybeans

Soybeans are the state's second-largest crop, and Iowa is the country's largest soy producer. Although 90 percent of the crop is used for animal feed, soybeans are a valuable source of protein and are used to make meat substitutes, such as tofu and other high-protein foods. In addition, soybeans are used to make hundreds of chemicals and medicines.

Food Processing

Iowa is situated around the middle of the United States. Its location makes it an ideal place for food processing plants, as products can be easily and quickly moved by truck or rail to many major cities across the country.

Limestone

Limestone is one source of Iowa's mining income. Limestone quarries are located in more than half the state's counties. The limestone is used for road construction and for manufacturing cement.

Iowa's tourism industry includes its nature preserves and wildlife refuges. Every year, many visitors come to Iowa to see the state's breathtaking landscapes.

The Future

The people of Iowa have taken imaginative steps to improve the quality of their lives. For example, Iowa experiences bitter cold spells in the winter, which makes it very hard for people to get out and have fun. Business leaders in Des Moines found a solution by helping to build a 4-mile (6.4 km) skywalk system. This enclosed walkway connects buildings in the downtown area. People can now walk to restaurants, shopping centers, offices, and theaters without ever stepping outside. Not only are people in Des Moines more comfortable in the winter, but businesses can continue to make money and support the economy. Iowans continue to work together to find ways to make their state the best it can be.

State Flag & Seal

Designed by an Iowa woman in 1917, the state flag has three vertical stripes—blue, white, and red. In the white center stripe an eagle carries in its beak blue streamers on which the state motto is inscribed: "Our liberties we prize, and our rights we will maintain."

The Great Seal of Iowa shows a citizen soldier standing in a field of wheat, surrounded by farm and industrial tools, with the Mississippi River in the background. Overhead, an eagle carries the state motto.

Iowa State Map

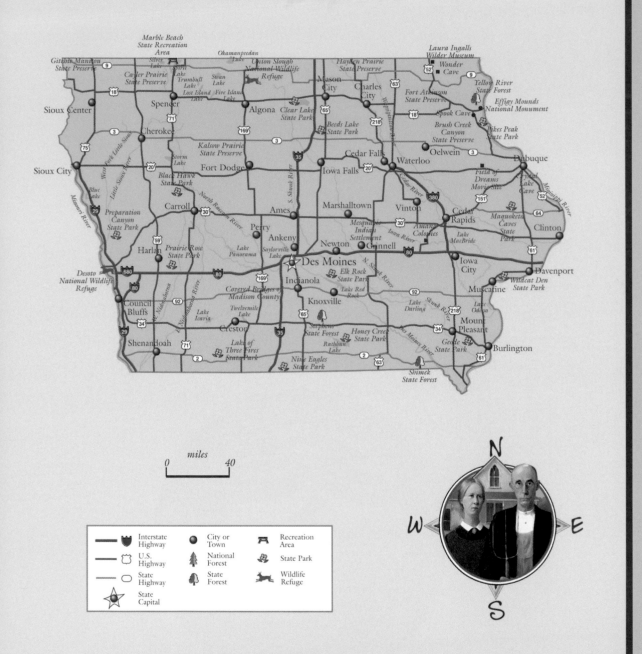

Gitchie Manitou State Preserve
Marble Beach State Recreation Area
Okamanpeedan Lake
Union Slough National Wildlife Refuge
Laura Ingalls Wilder Museum
Wonder Cave
Yellow River State Forest
Cayler Prairie State Preserve
Hayden Prairie State Preserve
Silver Lake
Spirit Lake
Trumbull Lake
Swan Lake
Five Island Lake
Lost Island Lake
Mason City
Charles City
Fort Atkinson State Preserve
Effigy Mounds National Monument
Spook Cave
Sioux Center
Spencer
Algona
Clear Lake State Park
Beeds Lake State Park
Brush Creek Canyon State Preserve
Pikes Peak State Park
Cherokee
Kalsow Prairie State Preserve
Cedar Falls
Oelwein
Dubuque
Sioux City
Storm Lake
Fort Dodge
Iowa Falls
Waterloo
Field of Dreams Movie Site
Crystal Lake Cave
Black Hawk State Park
Blue Lake
Preparation Canyon State Park
Carroll
Ames
Marshalltown
Vinton
Cedar Rapids
Maquoketa Caves State Park
Clinton
Perry
Mesquakie Indian Settlement
Amana Colonies
Lake MacBride
Harlan
Prairie Rose State Park
Lake Panorama
Ankeny
Saylorville Lake
Newton
Grinnell
Iowa City
Des Moines
Davenport
Desoto National Wildlife Refuge
Covered Bridges of Madison County
Indianola
Elk Rock State Park
Lake Red Rock
Muscatine
Wildcat Den State Park
Council Bluffs
Twelvemile Lake
Knoxville
Lake Darling
Lake Odessa
Mount Pleasant
Shenandoah
Creston
Lake Icaria
Lake of Three Fires State Park
Stephens State Forest
Rathbun Lake
Honey Creek State Park
Geode State Park
Burlington
Nine Eagles State Park
Shimek State Forest

miles
0   40

Legend

- Interstate Highway
- U.S. Highway
- State Highway
- State Capital
- City or Town
- National Forest
- State Forest
- Recreation Area
- State Park
- Wildlife Refuge

N
W   E
S

State Song

The Song of Iowa

words by Samuel Hawkins Marshall Byers

You ask what land I love the best, I - o-wa, 'tis I - o-wa, The
fair - est State of all the west, I - o-wa, O! I - o-wa. From
yon - der Mis - sis - sip - pi's stream To where Mis-sou - ri's wa - ters gleam O!
fair it is as po - et's dream, I - o-wa, in I - o-wa.

BOOKS

Balcavage, Dynise. *Iowa*. From Sea to Shining Sea. Danbury, CT: Children's Press, 2009.

Griggs, Howard. *The Native American Mound Builders*. Infomax Common Core Readers. New York: Rosen Classroom, 2014.

Schwieder, Dorothy, Thomas Morain, and Lynn Nielsen. *Iowa Past to Present: The People and the Prairie*. Iowa City, IA: University of Iowa Press, 2012.

WEBSITES

Iowa Fun Facts for Kids
http://factfinder2.census.gov/faces/nav/jsf/pages/index.xhtml

The Iowa Legislature
https://www.legis.iowa.gov/index.aspx

Official State of Iowa Website
http://www.iowa.gov/state/main/index.html

David C. King is an award-winning author who has written more than seventy books for children and young adults. He and his wife, Sharon, live in the Berkshires at the junction of New York, Massachusetts, and Connecticut. Their travels have taken them through most of the United States.